cooking for le$$

Pasta

Publications International, Ltd.
Favorite Brand Name Recipes at www.fbnr.com

Pictured on the front cover *(clockwise from top left):* Shells and Gorgonzola *(page 112),* Whole Wheat Penne with Broccoli and Sausage *(page 86),* Lentil Stew over Couscous *(page 36)* and Baked Gnocchi *(page 62).*

Pictured on the back cover *(left to right):* Manicotti *(page 66),* Gemelli & Grilled Summer Vegetables *(page 50)* and Turkey Vegetable Chili Mac *(page 8).*

ISBN-13: 978-1-4127-1677-2
ISBN-10: 1-4127-1677-2

Library of Congress Control Number: 2008933722

Manufactured in China.

8 7 6 5 4 3 2 1

Microwave Cooking: Microwave ovens vary in wattage. Use the cooking times as guidelines and check for doneness before adding more time.

Preparation/Cooking Times: Preparation times are based on the approximate amount of time required to assemble the recipe before cooking, baking, chilling or serving. These times include preparation steps such as measuring, chopping and mixing. The fact that some preparations and cooking can be done simultaneously is taken into account. Preparation of optional ingredients and serving suggestions is not included.

contents

HOW TO GET MORE OUT OF *COOKING FOR LESS*
Cutting back on your food bill shouldn't mean depriving yourself. With the recipes in this book and a few tips, you can eat better for less.

Supermarket Savvy
Think about the week ahead before you go shopping. Will half the family be home too late for dinner on Wednesday night? Will Thursday be so busy that you need to plan something extra quick and stress free? Jotting down the kinds of meals you'll need can save you from buying too much. Then make a grocery list and stick to it. It's easier to resist the colorful displays if you're prepared. It also helps to shop alone if possible, and it goes without saying that you should never, ever grocery shop when you're hungry!

Supermarkets are designed to get you to spend! Items are arranged so that you'll see enticing assortments of not-so-necessary goodies on your way to buy the milk and bread. Stick to the perimeter of the store as much as possible. That's where meat, produce and dairy are usually stocked. Read the sale flyers ahead of time while you're planning, and don't forget to bring along the coupons.

Beware of Bargains That Aren't
Do remember that the best price in the world on chicken livers isn't going to convince your family to eat them. Buying big, bargain sizes of items you know you'll use makes sense, but check the label posted on the shelf under the product. A giant economy size may look like a good deal, but sometimes it isn't. The small print listing cost per ounce may surprise you.

Healthy Budgeting

The good news is that eating more fruits and vegetables and less meat is better for your health as well as your wallet. Instead of just concentrating on meat as the centerpiece of a meal, consider what will go with it. You can stretch smaller portions of expensive protein with pasta, grains, rice and side dishes. You can take some cues from ethnic cooks, too. Asian dishes often use a small amount of chicken or beef to flavor a stir-fry that's mostly vegetables. Mexican cuisine counts on tortillas, rice and beans. Italians have pasta and pizza.

Add Flavor Instead of Dollars

Herbs and spices cost a lot per jar, but they can add huge amounts of flavor for only pennies. A little bit of mustard, balsamic vinegar or hot sauce can turn boring into mouthwatering. Stock up on flavorful pantry ingredients like these and you'll have lots of delicious options every time you cook.

Waste Less, Spend Less

Most of us end up discarding too much of the food we buy. (According to a government study, Americans waste one pound of food per day on average.) Think about what category your discards fall into and see if you can improve. Are you tossing vegetables that have rotted? Maybe you can shop more often or use frozen or canned. The kids don't clean their plates? Serve smaller portions and you can always refill them. You planned on making dinner, but life got in the way? You may be able to freeze ingredients or use them another way.

Pat Yourself on the Back

Cooking at home more and eating out less is a huge step in the right direction. It almost always saves money and provides more nutritious meals for your family. With a little creativity and planning, cooking for less can also be a delicious undertaking—and that's the best bargain of all!

hearty bowl food

RAVIOLI MINESTRONE

1 package (7 ounces) refrigerated three-cheese ravioli
2 teaspoons olive oil
2 carrots, chopped
1 stalk celery, chopped
1 medium onion, chopped
2 cloves garlic, minced
6 cups water
1 can (about 15 ounces) chickpeas, rinsed and drained
1 can (about 14 ounces) diced tomatoes
3 tablespoons tomato paste
1 teaspoon dried basil
1 teaspoon dried oregano
¾ teaspoon salt
¾ teaspoon black pepper
1 medium zucchini, halved lengthwise and sliced (about 2 cups)
1 package (10 ounces) baby spinach

1. Cook ravioli according to package directions; drain.

2. Meanwhile, heat oil in large Dutch oven over medium-high heat. Add carrots, celery, onion and garlic; cook and stir 5 minutes or until softened.

3. Stir in water, chickpeas, tomatoes, tomato paste, basil, oregano, salt and pepper. Bring to a boil; reduce heat and simmer 15 minutes or until vegetables are tender. Add zucchini; cook 5 minutes. Stir in spinach; cook 2 minutes or just until spinach wilts. Stir in ravioli.

Makes 8 servings

Prep Time: 20 minutes
Cook Time: 27 minutes

ravioli minestrone

TURKEY VEGETABLE CHILI MAC

Nonstick cooking spray
1 pound ground turkey
1 can (about 15 ounces) black beans, rinsed and drained
1 can (about 14 ounces) Mexican-style diced tomatoes
1 can (about 14 ounces) diced tomatoes
1 cup frozen corn
½ cup chopped onion
2 cloves garlic, minced
1 teaspoon Mexican seasoning
½ cup uncooked elbow macaroni
⅓ cup sour cream (optional)

Slow Cooker Directions

1. Spray large skillet with nonstick cooking spray. Add turkey; cook and stir 5 minutes or until browned.

2. Transfer turkey to 4-quart slow cooker. Add beans, tomatoes, corn, onion, garlic and seasoning. Cover; cook on LOW 4 to 5 hours.

3. Stir in macaroni. Cover; cook 30 to 40 minutes or until macaroni is tender, stirring after first 10 minutes. Serve with sour cream, if desired.

Makes 6 servings

turkey vegetable chili mac

ITALIAN BOW TIE VEGETABLE SOUP

3 cans (14½ ounces each) chicken broth
1 can (14½ ounces) Italian-style or regular stewed tomatoes
½ teaspoon Italian seasoning
1½ cups (4 ounces) uncooked bow tie pasta
1 package (about 1 pound) small frozen precooked meatballs
1 medium zucchini, cut into ¼-inch slices
½ cup diced red or green bell pepper
1½ cups *French's®* French Fried Onions

1. Combine broth, tomatoes and Italian seasoning in large saucepan. Bring to a boil.

2. Stir in pasta, meatballs, zucchini and bell pepper. Simmer for 12 minutes or until pasta is cooked al dente and meatballs are heated through, stirring occasionally. Spoon soup into serving bowls; top with French Fried Onions. *Makes 6 servings*

Prep Time: 5 minutes
Cook Time: 12 minutes

Frozen meatballs are an invaluable resource in the kitchen, saving both time and money. Look for them in bulk packaging through warehouse clubs or school fund-raising programs for even greater savings. Use them in sandwiches, casseroles and soups—or serve them over pasta for a quick and easy spaghetti dinner.

italian bow tie vegetable soup

RICH AND HEARTY DRUMSTICK SOUP

    2 turkey drumsticks (about 1¾ pounds total)
    3 carrots, peeled and sliced
    2 stalks celery, thinly sliced
    1 onion, chopped
    2 cloves garlic, minced
    1 teaspoon poultry seasoning
    1 container (32 ounces) chicken broth
    3 cups water
    8 ounces uncooked egg noodles
    ⅓ cup chopped fresh parsley (optional)
      Salt and black pepper

Slow Cooker Directions

1. Coat 5-quart slow cooker with nonstick cooking spray.

2. Place turkey, carrots, celery, onion, garlic and seasoning in slow cooker. Pour in broth and water. Cover; cook on HIGH 5 hours or until meat is falling off bones.

3. Remove turkey; set aside. Add noodles to slow cooker. Cover; cook 30 minutes or until noodles are tender. Meanwhile, remove and discard skin and bones from turkey; shred meat.

4. Return turkey to slow cooker; stir in parsley, if desired. Season with salt and pepper.   *Makes 8 servings*

rich and hearty drumstick soup

SPICY LENTIL AND PASTA SOUP

1 tablespoon olive oil
2 medium onions, thinly sliced
½ cup chopped carrot
½ cup chopped celery
½ cup peeled and chopped turnip
1 jalapeño pepper,* seeded and finely chopped
2 cans (about 14 ounces each) vegetable broth
2 cups water
1 can (about 14 ounces) stewed tomatoes
8 ounces dried lentils, rinsed and sorted
2 teaspoons chili powder
½ teaspoon dried oregano
3 ounces uncooked whole wheat spaghetti, broken
¼ cup minced fresh cilantro (optional)

*Jalapeño peppers can sting and irritate the skin, so wear rubber gloves when handling peppers and do not touch your eyes.

1. Heat oil in large saucepan over medium heat. Add onions, carrot, celery, turnip and jalapeño pepper; cook and stir 10 minutes or until vegetables are crisp-tender.

2. Add broth, water, tomatoes, lentils, chili powder and oregano; bring to a boil. Reduce heat; simmer, covered, 20 to 30 minutes or until lentils are tender.

3. Add pasta; cook 10 minutes or until tender.

4. Ladle soup into bowls; sprinkle with cilantro, if desired.

Makes 6 servings

TOMATO AND TURKEY SOUP WITH PESTO

1 cup uncooked rotini pasta
2 cups frozen Italian-style vegetables
1 can (10¾ ounces) condensed tomato soup, undiluted
1 cup milk
2 tablespoons prepared pesto
1 cup chopped cooked turkey
2 tablespoons grated Parmesan cheese

1. Cook pasta according to package directions; drain.

2. Meanwhile, combine vegetables, soup, milk and pesto in medium saucepan. Bring to a boil over medium-high heat; reduce heat to low. Simmer, partially covered, 10 minutes or until vegetables are tender. Add pasta and turkey. Cook 3 minutes or until heated through. Sprinkle with cheese just before serving.   *Makes 4 servings*

CREAMY CHEDDAR CHEESE SOUP

2 cans (10¾ ounces each) condensed Cheddar cheese soup
3 cups milk or water
3 cups cooked vegetables, such as cauliflower, carrots and asparagus,
    cut into bite-size pieces
2 cups cooked medium shell pasta
1⅓ cups *French's®* French Fried Onions

Combine soup and milk in large saucepan. Stir in vegetables and pasta. Bring to a boil. Reduce heat. Cook until heated through, stirring often.

Place French Fried Onions on microwavable dish. Microwave on HIGH 1 minute or until onions are golden.

Ladle soup into individual bowls. Sprinkle with onions.
                                           Makes 6 servings

Prep Time: 10 minutes
Cook Time: 5 minutes

PASTA FAGIOLI

1 jar (1 pound 10 ounces) RAGÚ® Chunky Gardenstyle Pasta Sauce
1 can (19 ounces) white kidney beans, rinsed and drained
1 box (10 ounces) frozen chopped spinach, thawed
8 ounces ditalini pasta, cooked and drained (reserve 2 cups pasta water)

1. In 6-quart saucepot, combine Pasta Sauce, beans, spinach, pasta and reserved pasta water; heat through.

2. Season, if desired, with salt, ground black pepper and grated Parmesan cheese. *Makes 4 servings*

Prep Time: 20 minutes
Cook Time: 10 minutes

HEARTY FETTUCCINE, HAM AND BEAN SOUP

2 tablespoons olive oil
1 cup canned chunky Italian tomato sauce
1 cup diced cooked ham
2 cloves garlic, chopped
4 cups canned fat-free low-sodium chicken broth, divided
1 (15-ounce) can garbanzo beans, drained, divided
4 ounces fettuccine (broken into thirds), elbows or rotini pasta
  Parmesan cheese

Heat oil in saucepan over medium heat. Add tomato sauce, ham and garlic. Simmer 5 minutes. Add 3 cups broth; stir to blend. Purée remaining broth and 1 cup garbanzo beans in blender. Add to saucepan; add remaining garbanzo beans. Bring to a boil, reduce heat and simmer 10 minutes. Add pasta; cook until tender, about 10 minutes. Serve, passing Parmesan cheese separately. *Makes 4 to 6 servings*

Favorite recipe from *North Dakota Wheat Commission*

ITALIAN SAUSAGE SOUP

1 pound mild Italian sausage, casings removed
½ cup plain dry bread crumbs
¼ cup grated Parmesan cheese
¼ cup milk
1 egg
½ teaspoon dried basil
½ teaspoon black pepper
¼ teaspoon garlic salt
4 cups hot chicken broth
1 tablespoon tomato paste
1 clove garlic, minced
¼ teaspoon red pepper flakes
½ cup small shell, mini bowtie or ditalini pasta
1 bag (10 ounces) baby spinach
Additional grated Parmesan cheese (optional)

Slow Cooker Directions

1. Combine sausage, bread crumbs, ¼ cup cheese, milk, egg, basil, black pepper and garlic salt in large bowl. Shape into marble-size balls.

2. Combine broth, tomato paste, garlic and pepper flakes in 4-quart slow cooker. Add meatballs. Cover; cook on LOW 5 to 6 hours.

3. Stir in pasta 30 minutes before serving. When pasta is tender, stir in spinach. Sprinkle with additional cheese, if desired, and serve immediately. *Makes 4 to 6 servings*

Prep Time: 15 minutes
Cook Time: 5 to 6 hours

PIZZA MEATBALL AND NOODLE SOUP

1 can (about 14 ounces) beef broth
½ cup chopped onion
½ cup chopped carrot
2 ounces uncooked whole wheat spaghetti, broken
½ medium zucchini, halved lengthwise and thinly sliced
8 ounces frozen fully-cooked Italian-style meatballs, thawed
1 can (8 ounces) tomato sauce
½ cup (2 ounces) shredded mozzarella cheese

1. Combine broth, onion and carrot in large saucepan. Add spaghetti. Bring to a boil. Reduce heat; cover and simmer 3 minutes.

2. Add zucchini, meatballs and tomato sauce to broth mixture. Return to a boil. Reduce heat; cover and simmer 8 to 9 minutes or until meatballs are heated through and spaghetti is tender, stirring frequently. Ladle into bowls. Sprinkle with cheese.   *Makes 2 to 4 servings*

Prep Time: 15 minutes

Soups and stews are a great way to stretch your food budget. These recipes are usually forgiving enough that they can be halved or doubled with ease based on your needs. Soups and stews freeze beautifully, making it easy to prepare large batches that can be defrosted later for quick lunches or dinners. They are also a great way to use up leftover meat, vegetables, rice or beans from other meals and recipes.

pizza meatball and noodle soup

EASY TOMATO MINESTRONE

  3 slices bacon, diced
½ cup chopped onion
  1 clove garlic, minced
3½ cups water
  2 cans (10½ ounces each) condensed beef broth, undiluted
  1 can (15 ounces) Great Northern beans, undrained
  1 can (6 ounces) CONTADINA® Tomato Paste
½ cup dry pasta shells, macaroni or vermicelli, broken into 1-inch pieces
¼ cup chopped fresh parsley
  1 teaspoon dried oregano leaves, crushed
  1 teaspoon dried basil leaves, crushed
¼ teaspoon black pepper
  1 package (16 ounces) frozen mixed Italian vegetables
½ cup grated Parmesan cheese (optional)

1. Sauté bacon, onion and garlic in large saucepan until onion is translucent.

2. Stir in water, broth, beans and liquid, tomato paste, pasta, parsley, oregano, basil and pepper; heat to boiling.

3. Reduce heat; simmer 15 minutes. Mix in vegetables; cook additional 10 minutes. Serve with Parmesan cheese, if desired.

Makes about 8 servings

easy tomato minestrone

HEARTY PASTA AND CHICKPEA CHOWDER

6 ounces uncooked rotini pasta
6 slices bacon
2 tablespoons olive oil
¾ cup chopped onion
½ cup thinly sliced carrot
½ cup chopped celery
2 cloves garlic, minced
¼ cup all-purpose flour
1½ teaspoons Italian seasoning
⅛ teaspoon red pepper flakes
⅛ teaspoon black pepper
2 cans (about 14 ounces each) chicken broth
1 can (about 15 ounces) chickpeas, rinsed and drained
1 can (about 14 ounces) Italian-style stewed tomatoes

1. Cook pasta according to package directions; drain.

2. Place bacon between double layer of paper towels on paper plate. Microwave on HIGH 5 to 6 minutes or until bacon is crisp. Drain and crumble.

3. Heat oil in 4-quart Dutch oven over medium heat. Add onion, carrot, celery and garlic. Cook and stir 5 to 6 minutes or until vegetables are crisp-tender.

4. Remove from heat. Stir in flour, seasoning, pepper flakes and black pepper until well blended. Gradually stir in broth. Bring to a boil over high heat, stirring frequently. Boil 1 minute, stirring constantly. Reduce heat to medium. Stir in pasta, chickpeas and tomatoes. Cook 5 minutes or until heated through.

5. Ladle chowder into bowls; sprinkle with bacon. Serve immediately.

Makes 6 servings

Prep and Cook Time: 30 minutes

ONION SOUP WITH PASTA

 2 tablespoons olive oil
 3 cups sliced onions
 3 cloves garlic, minced
 ½ teaspoon sugar
 2 cans (about 14 ounces each) beef broth
 ½ cup uncooked small star pasta
 2 tablespoons dry sherry (optional)
 ⅛ teaspoon black pepper
   Grated Parmesan cheese (optional)

1. Heat oil in large saucepan over medium heat; add onions and garlic. Cook, covered, 5 to 8 minutes or until onions are softened. Stir in sugar; cook 15 minutes or until onion mixture is very soft and browned.

2. Add broth to saucepan; bring to a boil. Add pasta and simmer, uncovered, 6 to 8 minutes or until tender. Stir in sherry, if desired, and pepper. Ladle soup into bowls. Sprinkle with cheese, if desired.

Makes 4 servings

To vary the flavor of this soup, try using a mixture of white, yellow and sweet onions. To get the most value out of this budget-friendly soup, review supermarket and produce center sale flyers before shopping and use whichever variety is least expensive that week.

ITALIAN VEGETABLE STEW

1 teaspoon olive oil
2 medium zucchini, halved lengthwise and thinly sliced
1 medium eggplant, chopped
1 large onion, thinly sliced
1/8 teaspoon ground black pepper
1 jar (1 pound 10 ounces) RAGÚ® Light Pasta Sauce
3 tablespoons grated Parmesan cheese
1 box (10 ounces) couscous

1. In 12-inch nonstick skillet, heat olive oil over medium heat. Cook zucchini, eggplant, onion and pepper, stirring occasionally, 15 minutes or until vegetables are golden.

2. Stir in Pasta Sauce and cheese. Bring to a boil over high heat. Reduce heat to low and simmer covered 10 minutes.

3. Meanwhile, prepare couscous according to package directions. Serve vegetable mixture over hot couscous. *Makes 4 servings*

Prep Time: 10 minutes
Cook Time: 25 minutes

italian vegetable stew

HEARTY BEAN & PASTA SOUP

1 cup uncooked elbow macaroni
2 tablespoons olive oil
1 medium onion, chopped
2 cloves garlic, minced
4 cups water
2 cans (about 14 ounces each) chicken broth
1 jar (26 ounces) marinara sauce
1 can (about 15 ounces) Great Northern or cannellini beans,
   rinsed and drained
1 pound spinach, stemmed and chopped
2 teaspoons balsamic vinegar
½ cup grated Parmesan cheese (optional)

1. Cook macaroni according to package directions; drain.

2. Meanwhile, heat oil in Dutch oven or large saucepan over medium heat. Add onion and garlic; cook and stir 5 minutes or until onion is tender.

3. Stir in water, broth, marinara sauce and beans; bring to a boil. Reduce heat to low; simmer 10 minutes, stirring occasionally. Stir in spinach, vinegar and pasta; cook 5 minutes.

4. Ladle soup into bowls; sprinkle with cheese, if desired. Serve immediately.   *Makes 10 to 12 servings*

vegetable harvest

HOMEMADE SPINACH RAVIOLI

1 package (10 ounces) frozen chopped spinach, thawed and
   squeezed dry
1 cup ricotta cheese
½ cup grated Romano or Parmesan cheese
1 egg
1 tablespoon minced fresh basil *or* 1 teaspoon dried basil
½ teaspoon salt
½ teaspoon black pepper
¼ teaspoon ground nutmeg
36 wonton wrappers
1 jar (about 26 ounces) marinara or other pasta sauce

1. For filling, combine spinach, cheeses, egg, basil, salt, pepper and
nutmeg in medium bowl.

2. Place 2 wonton wrappers on lightly floured surface, keeping
remaining wrappers covered. Place 1 heaping teaspoonful filling
in center of each wrapper. Moisten edges around filling and place
another wrapper on top. Press edges gently around filling to remove air
bubbles and seal. (If using square wrappers, cut with 1½-inch round
or scalloped cookie cutter to make circle, if desired.) Repeat with
remaining wrappers. (Any leftover filling may be frozen for later use.)

3. Bring large saucepan of salted water to a boil. Meanwhile, heat
marinara sauce in medium saucepan over low heat. Add half of ravioli
to boiling water; reduce heat to medium-high. Cook 3 minutes or until
ravioli rise to top. Remove ravioli with slotted spoon and keep warm.
Repeat with remaining ravioli. Serve with marinara sauce.

Makes 4 servings

homemade spinach ravioli

RATATOUILLE WITH PENNE

1 can (10¾ ounces) CAMPBELL'S® Condensed Tomato Soup (Regular *or* Healthy Request)
1 tablespoon olive oil
⅛ teaspoon ground black pepper
1 small eggplant, peeled and cut into ½-inch cubes (about 5 cups)
1 medium zucchini, thinly sliced (about 1½ cups)
1 medium red pepper, diced (about 1 cup)
1 large onion, sliced (about 1 cup)
1 clove garlic, minced
  Tube-shaped pasta (penne), cooked and drained
  Grated Parmesan cheese

1. Stir the soup, olive oil, black pepper, eggplant, zucchini, red pepper, onion and garlic in 4- to 5½-quart slow cooker.

2. Cover and cook on LOW 5½ to 6 hours* or until vegetables are tender.

3. Serve over the pasta with the cheese. *Makes 4 servings*

*Or on HIGH 2½ to 3 hours.

Tip: Serve with PEPPERIDGE FARM® Hot & Crusty Italian Bread.

Prep Time: 15 minutes
Cook Time: 5½ to 6 hours

ratatouille with penne

CREAMY FETTUCCINE WITH ASPARAGUS & LIMA BEANS

8 ounces uncooked fettuccine
2 tablespoons butter
2 cups asparagus pieces (about 1 inch long)
1 cup frozen lima beans, thawed
¼ teaspoon black pepper
½ cup vegetable broth
1 cup half-and-half or whipping cream
1 cup grated Parmesan cheese

1. Cook fettuccine according to package directions. Drain; keep warm.

2. Meanwhile, melt butter in large skillet over medium-high heat. Add asparagus, lima beans and pepper; cook and stir 3 minutes. Add broth; simmer 3 minutes. Add half-and-half; simmer 3 to 4 minutes or until vegetables are tender.

3. Add vegetable mixture and cheese to fettuccine; toss well. Serve immediately. *Makes 4 servings*

THREE BEAN & PASTA SALAD

8 ounces rotelle or spiral pasta
1 can (15 ounces) red kidney beans, rinsed and drained
1 can (15 ounces) chickpeas, rinsed and drained
1 cup fresh or frozen thawed green beans
¾ cup WISH-BONE® Italian Dressing
1 tablespoon lemon juice
1 tablespoon chopped fresh cilantro or parsley

1. Cook rotelle according to package directions; drain and rinse with cold water until completely cool.

2. In large bowl, toss cooked rotelle with remaining ingredients. Chill, if desired. *Makes 4 servings*

**creamy fettuccine with asparagus
& lima beans**

LENTIL STEW OVER COUSCOUS

3 cups (1 pound) dried lentils, rinsed and sorted
3 cups water
1 can (about 14 ounces) diced tomatoes
1 can (about 14 ounces) vegetable broth
1 large onion, chopped
1 green bell pepper, chopped
4 stalks celery, chopped
1 medium carrot, halved lengthwise and sliced
2 cloves garlic, chopped
1 teaspoon dried marjoram
¼ teaspoon black pepper
1 tablespoon cider vinegar
1 tablespoon olive oil
4½ to 5 cups hot cooked couscous

Slow Cooker Directions

1. Combine lentils, water, tomatoes, broth, onion, bell pepper, celery, carrot, garlic, marjoram and black pepper in 5-quart slow cooker. Stir; cover and cook on LOW 8 to 9 hours or until vegetables are tender.

2. Stir in vinegar and olive oil. Serve over couscous.

Makes 12 servings

Making large batches of soups and stews on the weekend is both economical and a great way to put dinner on the table quickly during the week. Lentil stew keeps well in the refrigerator for up to 1 week. It can also be portioned out into airtight containers and frozen for up to three months.

lentil stew over couscous

SPICY ORZO AND BLACK BEAN SALAD

2 tablespoons olive oil
2 tablespoons minced jalapeño pepper,* divided
1 teaspoon chili powder
6 cups water
¾ cup uncooked orzo pasta
1 cup frozen mixed vegetables
1 can (about 15 ounces) black beans, rinsed and drained
2 thin slices red onion
¼ cup chopped fresh cilantro
¼ cup fresh lime juice
¼ cup fresh lemon juice
4 cups torn stemmed spinach
2 tablespoons crumbled blue cheese (optional)

*Jalapeño peppers can sting and irritate the skin, so wear rubber gloves when handling peppers and do not touch your eyes.

1. Combine oil, 1 tablespoon jalapeño pepper and chili powder in medium bowl; set aside.

2. Bring water and remaining 1 tablespoon jalapeño to a boil in large saucepan. Add pasta. Cook 10 to 12 minutes or until tender; drain. Rinse in cold water; drain.

3. Place frozen vegetables in small microwavable dish. Cover; microwave on HIGH 3 minutes or until heated through. Let stand 5 minutes.

4. Add pasta, vegetables, beans, onion, cilantro, lime juice and lemon juice to oil mixture; toss to coat. Divide spinach evenly among serving plates. Top with pasta mixture. Sprinkle with cheese, if desired.

Makes 2 to 4 servings

Prep and Cook Time: 25 minutes

BOWTIES WITH ZUCCHINI

1 package (16 ounces) uncooked bowtie pasta
¼ cup vegetable oil
1 cup chopped onion
2 cloves garlic, minced
5 small zucchini, cut into thin strips
⅔ cup whipping cream
3 tablespoons grated Parmesan cheese
   Salt and black pepper

1. Preheat oven to 350°F.

2. Cook pasta according to package directions; drain.

3. Heat oil in large skillet over medium-high heat. Add onion and garlic; cook and stir 3 minutes or until onion is translucent. Add zucchini; cook and stir 5 minutes or until tender.

4. Add cream; cook and stir 2 minutes or until thickened. Add pasta and cheese to skillet. Season with salt and pepper.

5. Transfer mixture to 2-quart casserole. Cover and bake 15 minutes or until heated through. *Makes 8 servings*

OLIVE AND BROCCOLI SALAD WITH ITALIAN TOMATO DRESSING

10 ounces dry rotini or bowtie pasta
1 can (6 ounces) CONTADINA® Tomato Paste
1 cup Italian dressing
½ teaspoon hot pepper sauce
3 cups broccoli flowerets, cooked
1 cup halved pitted ripe olives, drained
1 medium red onion, cut into thin strips
½ cup diced cucumber
2 tablespoons pine nuts, toasted

1. Cook pasta according to package directions; drain and chill.

2. Meanwhile, combine tomato paste, dressing and hot pepper sauce in small bowl.

3. Combine pasta, broccoli, olives, onion and cucumber in large bowl; toss well. Add tomato paste mixture; mix lightly. Transfer salad to platter; sprinkle with pine nuts. *Makes 8 servings*

Prep Time: 10 minutes
Cook Time: 12 minutes

Pine nuts add flavor and crunch to this dish, however they are often quite expensive. Buy the smallest quantity you can find and store any leftover pine nuts in a resealable food storage bag or airtight container. Refrigerate up to 3 months or freeze up to 9 months. They can also be omitted from the recipe, if necessary.

olive and broccoli salad with
italian tomato dressing

MEDITERRANEAN ORZO AND VEGETABLE PILAF

¾ cup uncooked orzo pasta
2 teaspoons olive oil
1 small onion, diced
2 cloves garlic, minced
1 small zucchini, diced
½ cup vegetable broth
1 can (about 14 ounces) artichoke hearts, drained and quartered
1 medium tomato, chopped
½ teaspoon dried oregano
½ teaspoon salt
¼ teaspoon black pepper
½ cup crumbled feta cheese (optional)
   Sliced black olives (optional)

1. Cook pasta according to package directions; drain.

2. Heat oil in large nonstick skillet over medium heat. Add onion; cook and stir 5 minutes or until tender. Add garlic; cook and stir 1 minute.

3. Add zucchini and broth to skillet. Reduce heat; simmer 5 minutes or until zucchini is crisp-tender.

4. Add pasta, artichokes, tomato, oregano, salt and pepper to skillet; cook and stir 2 minutes or until heated through. Sprinkle with cheese and olives, if desired.   *Makes 2 servings*

Prep Time: 15 minutes
Cook Time: 10 minutes

mediterranean orzo and vegetable pilaf

VEGGIE NO BOILING LASAGNA

1 tablespoon olive oil
1 medium sweet onion, thinly sliced
1 medium red bell pepper, thinly sliced
1 medium zucchini, cut in half lengthwise and thinly sliced
2 containers (15 ounces each) ricotta cheese
2 cups shredded mozzarella cheese (about 8 ounces), divided
½ cup grated Parmesan cheese, divided
2 eggs
2 jars (1 pound 10 ounces each) RAGÚ® Old World Style® Pasta Sauce
12 uncooked lasagna noodles

1. Preheat oven to 375°F. In 12-inch nonstick skillet, heat olive oil over medium-high heat and cook onion, red bell pepper and zucchini, stirring occasionally, 5 minutes or until softened.

2. Meanwhile, combine ricotta cheese, 1 cup mozzarella cheese, ¼ cup Parmesan cheese and eggs.

3. In 13×9-inch baking dish, spread 1 cup Pasta Sauce. Layer 4 uncooked noodles, then 1 cup Sauce, half of ricotta mixture and half of vegetables; repeat. Top with remaining uncooked noodles and 2 cups Sauce. Reserve remaining Sauce.

4. Cover with foil and bake 1 hour. Remove foil; sprinkle with remaining cheeses. Bake uncovered 10 minutes. Let stand 10 minutes before serving. Serve with reserved Pasta Sauce, heated.

Makes 12 servings

Prep Time: 15 minutes
Cook Time: 1 hour, 15 minutes

PASTA AND POTATOES WITH PESTO

3 medium unpeeled red potatoes, cut into chunks
8 ounces uncooked linguine
¾ cup frozen peas
1 package (about 7 ounces) prepared pesto
¼ cup plus 2 tablespoons grated Parmesan cheese, divided
¼ teaspoon salt
¼ teaspoon black pepper

1. Place potatoes in medium saucepan; cover with water. Bring to a boil over high heat; reduce heat. Simmer 10 minutes or until potatoes are tender; drain.

2. Meanwhile, cook linguine according to package directions, adding peas during last 3 minutes of cooking. Drain; return pasta mixture to saucepan.

3. Add potatoes, pesto, ¼ cup cheese, salt and pepper to pasta. Toss until blended.

4. Sprinkle with remaining 2 tablespoons cheese. Serve immediately.

Makes 6 servings

pasta and potatoes with pesto

STUFFED SHELLS WITH VEGETABLES BOLOGNESE SAUCE

1 container (15 ounces) ricotta cheese
1 cup shredded mozzarella cheese (about 8 ounces)
¼ cup grated Parmesan cheese
1 tablespoon olive oil
1 large sweet onion, finely chopped
1 medium zucchini, chopped
1 large carrot, chopped
1 medium red or orange bell pepper, chopped
1 jar (1 pound 10 ounces) RAGÚ® Old World Style® Meat Pasta Sauce
2 cups chopped baby spinach leaves
1 box jumbo shells pasta (about 24 shells), cooked and drained

1. Preheat oven to 350°F. In medium bowl, combine ricotta, ½ cup mozzarella and Parmesan cheese; set aside.

2. In 4-quart saucepan, heat olive oil over medium-high heat and cook onion, zucchini, carrot and red pepper, stirring occasionally, 5 minutes or until vegetables are tender. Stir in Meat Pasta Sauce. Bring to a boil over high heat. Stir in spinach. Reduce heat to low and simmer, stirring occasionally, 5 minutes.

3. Meanwhile, evenly stuff shells with cheese mixture. In 13×9-inch baking dish sprayed with nonstick cooking spray, arrange shells. Pour sauce mixture over shells. Sprinkle with remaining ½ cup mozzarella cheese.

4. Bake, covered, 30 minutes or until heated through and cheese is melted. *Makes 8 servings*

Prep Time: 30 minutes
Cook Time: 45 minutes

CHICKPEA PASTA SALAD

4 ounces uncooked spinach rotini or fusilli pasta
1 can (about 15 ounces) chickpeas, rinsed and drained
½ cup chopped red bell pepper
⅓ cup chopped celery
⅓ cup finely chopped carrot
2 green onions, chopped
3 tablespoons balsamic vinegar
2 tablespoons mayonnaise
2 teaspoons coarse grain mustard
½ teaspoon black pepper
¼ teaspoon Italian seasoning
   Cherry tomatoes (optional)

1. Cook pasta according to package directions; drain. Rinse under cold water until cool; drain.

2. Combine pasta, chickpeas, bell pepper, celery, carrot and green onions in medium bowl.

3. Whisk together vinegar, mayonnaise, mustard, black pepper and seasoning in small bowl. Pour over salad; toss to coat evenly. Cover and refrigerate up to 8 hours. Garnish with cherry tomatoes.

Makes 4 servings

Chickpeas and other beans are an excellent source of protein, calcium and iron and an inexpensive substitute for meat. Stock up on canned beans when they are on sale so you always have these pantry staples on hand. To save even more money, purchase dried beans in bulk where available. Prepare them in advance and freeze them in small portions in freezer food storage bags. These can be used in place of canned beans in all recipes.

GEMELLI & GRILLED SUMMER VEGETABLES

2 bell peppers
1 bunch asparagus, trimmed
1 red onion, thickly sliced
3 tablespoons plus 1 teaspoon olive oil, divided
8 ounces uncooked gemelli or rotini pasta
2 tablespoons pine nuts
1 clove garlic
1 cup loosely packed fresh basil leaves
¼ cup grated Parmesan cheese
¼ teaspoon salt
¼ teaspoon black pepper
1 cup grape or cherry tomatoes

1. Prepare grill for direct cooking. Cut bell peppers in half; remove and discard seeds. Place peppers, skin side down, on grid over medium heat. Grill, covered, 10 to 12 minutes or until skins are blackened. Place peppers in paper or plastic bag; let stand 15 minutes. Remove and discard blackened skins. Cut peppers into chunks. Place in large bowl.

2. Toss asparagus and onion with 1 teaspoon oil. Grill, covered, 8 to 10 minutes or until tender, turning once. Cut asparagus into 2-inch pieces and coarsely chop onion; add to peppers.

3. Cook pasta according to package directions; drain. Add pasta to vegetables.

4. Process pine nuts and garlic in food processor until coarsely chopped. Add basil; process until finely chopped. While processor is running, add remaining 3 tablespoons oil. Stir in cheese, salt and black pepper. Add basil mixture and tomatoes to pasta mixture; toss to coat. Serve immediately. *Makes 6 servings*

gemelli & grilled summer vegetables

SPICY PEANUT NOODLE SALAD

⅓ cup *French's*® Honey Dijon Mustard
⅓ cup reduced-sodium chicken broth
⅓ cup peanut butter
2 tablespoons reduced-sodium teriyaki sauce
2 tablespoons *Frank's*® *RedHot*® Cayenne Pepper Sauce, or more to taste
2 cups thinly sliced vegetables, such as green onion, snow peas, cucumber or bell peppers
4 ounces thin spaghetti, cooked and drained (1½ cups cooked)

1. Combine mustard, chicken broth, peanut butter, teriyaki sauce and *Frank's*® *RedHot*® Sauce in large bowl; whisk until blended.

2. Add remaining ingredients; toss to coat. Serve immediately. If desired, serve on salad greens. *Makes 4 servings*

Tip: To serve as a main dish, add 2 cups diced cooked turkey.

Prep Time: 10 minutes

Although they come in large containers and are only called for in small amounts in this recipe, pantry staples like mustard, teriyaki sauce and peanut butter are worth the investment. They add serious flavor even when used sparingly, have a long shelf-life when refrigerated and can be used in a wide variety of dishes. Buy quality brands when they are on sale and you will notice a difference in your finished dishes.

spicy peanut noodle salad

BROCCOLI–CHEESE STUFFED SHELLS

1 container (15 ounces) ricotta cheese
1 package (10 ounces) frozen chopped broccoli, thawed and well
    drained
1 cup shredded mozzarella cheese (4 ounces)
⅓ cup grated Parmesan cheese
¼ teaspoon black pepper
18 jumbo pasta shells, cooked and drained
1 jar (1 pound 9.75 ounces) PREGO® Garden Combination Italian Sauce

1. Stir the ricotta cheese, broccoli, ½ **cup** of the mozzarella cheese, Parmesan cheese and black pepper in a medium bowl. Spoon **about 2 tablespoons** of the cheese mixture into **each** shell.

2. Spread **1 cup** of the sauce in a 13×9×2-inch (3-quart) shallow baking dish. Place the filled shells on the sauce. Pour the remaining sauce over the shells. Sprinkle with the remaining mozzarella cheese.

3. Bake at 400°F. for 25 minutes or until hot.   *Makes 6 servings*

Tip: To thaw the broccoli, microwave on HIGH 4 minutes.

Prep Time: 25 minutes
Cook Time: 25 minutes

broccoli-cheese stuffed shells

oven-baked favorites

BAKED RIGATONI

1 pound dry rigatoni
4 ounces mild Italian sausage, casings removed, sliced
1 cup chopped onion
2 cloves garlic, minced
1 can (14.5 ounces) CONTADINA® Recipe Ready Diced Tomatoes, undrained
1 can (6 ounces) CONTADINA Tomato Paste
1 cup chicken broth
1 teaspoon salt
1 cup (4 ounces) shredded mozzarella cheese, divided
½ cup (2 ounces) shredded Parmesan cheese (optional)
2 tablespoons chopped fresh basil *or* 2 teaspoons dried basil leaves, crushed

1. Cook pasta according to package directions. Drain and keep warm.

2. Meanwhile, cook sausage in large skillet for 4 to 6 minutes or until no longer pink. Remove sausage from skillet, reserving any drippings in skillet.

3. Add onion and garlic to skillet; sauté for 2 minutes. Stir in undrained tomatoes, tomato paste, broth and salt.

4. Bring to a boil. Reduce heat to low; simmer, uncovered, for 10 minutes, stirring occasionally.

5. Combine pasta, tomato mixture, sausage, ½ cup mozzarella cheese, Parmesan cheese and basil in large bowl; spoon into ungreased 13×9-inch baking dish. Sprinkle with remaining mozzarella cheese.

6. Bake in preheated 375°F oven for 10 to 15 minutes or until cheese is melted.

Makes 8 servings

Prep Time: 10 minutes
Cook Time: 33 minutes

baked rigatoni

CRAB–ARTICHOKE CASSEROLE

8 ounces uncooked small shell pasta
2 tablespoons butter
6 green onions, chopped
2 tablespoons all-purpose flour
1 cup half-and-half
1 teaspoon dry mustard
½ teaspoon ground red pepper
   Salt and black pepper
½ cup (2 ounces) shredded Swiss cheese, divided
1 package (about 8 ounces) imitation crabmeat
1 can (about 14 ounces) artichoke hearts, drained and cut into
   bite-size pieces

1. Preheat oven to 350°F. Grease 2-quart casserole. Cook pasta according to package directions until almost tender; drain.

2. Melt butter in large saucepan over medium heat. Add green onions; cook and stir 2 minutes. Add flour; cook and stir 2 minutes. Gradually add half-and-half, whisking constantly until mixture begins to thicken. Whisk in mustard and red pepper. Season with salt and black pepper. Remove from heat; stir in ¼ cup cheese until melted.

3. Combine crabmeat, artichokes and pasta in prepared casserole. Add sauce mixture; stir until blended. Top with remaining ¼ cup cheese. Bake 40 minutes or until bubbly and cheese is melted.

Makes 6 servings

This tasty casserole can also be made with leftover chicken from another meal. The rich creamy sauce, tangy Swiss cheese and tender artichoke hearts will transform simple roasted chicken into a second delicious dinner.

crab-artichoke casserole

CHEESY TUNA NOODLE CASSEROLE

1 can (10¾ ounces) CAMPBELL'S® Condensed Cream of Mushroom Soup
   (Regular *or* 98% Fat Free)
½ cup milk
1 cup frozen peas
2 cans (about 6 ounces each) tuna, drained and flaked
2 cups hot cooked medium egg noodles
½ cup shredded Cheddar cheese

1. Stir the soup, milk, peas, tuna and noodles in a 1½-quart casserole.

2. Bake at 400°F. for 20 minutes or until hot. Stir.

3. Sprinkle cheese over the tuna mixture. Bake for 2 minutes more or until the cheese melts.   *Makes 4 servings*

Easy Substitution Tip: Substitute your family's favorite frozen vegetable for the peas.

Prep Time: 10 minutes
Bake Time: 22 minutes

cheesy tuna noodle casserole

BAKED GNOCCHI

1 package (about 17 ounces) gnocchi (frozen or vacuum-packed)
⅓ cup olive oil
3 cloves garlic, minced
1 package (10 ounces) frozen spinach, thawed and squeezed dry
1 can (about 14 ounces) diced tomatoes
1 teaspoon Italian seasoning
  Salt and black pepper
½ cup grated Parmesan cheese
½ cup (2 ounces) shredded mozzarella cheese

1. Preheat oven to 350°F. Grease large casserole.

2. Cook gnocchi according to package directions; drain.

3. Meanwhile, heat oil in large heavy skillet or Dutch oven over medium heat. Add garlic; cook and stir 30 seconds. Stir in spinach. Cook, covered, 2 minutes or until spinach wilts. Add tomatoes and seasoning. Season with salt and pepper; cook and stir 5 minutes. Add gnocchi; stir gently.

4. Transfer gnocchi mixture to prepared casserole. Sprinkle with Parmesan and mozzarella cheeses. Bake 20 to 30 minutes or until bubbly and cheese is melted.   *Makes 4 to 6 servings*

baked gnocchi

HUNGARIAN GOULASH CASSEROLE

1 pound ground pork
¼ teaspoon salt
¼ teaspoon ground nutmeg
¼ teaspoon black pepper
1 tablespoon vegetable oil
1 cup sour cream, divided
1 tablespoon cornstarch
1 can (10¾ ounces) condensed cream of celery soup, undiluted
1 cup milk
1 teaspoon sweet Hungarian paprika
1 package (12 ounces) egg noodles, cooked and drained
2 teaspoons minced fresh dill (optional)

1. Preheat oven to 325°F. Spray 3-quart casserole with nonstick cooking spray.

2. Combine pork, salt, nutmeg and pepper in medium bowl. Shape into 1-inch balls. Heat oil in large skillet over medium-high heat. Add meatballs; cook and stir 10 minutes or until browned on all sides and no longer pink in center. Remove meatballs from skillet; drain fat.

3. Stir together ¼ cup sour cream and cornstarch in small bowl. Combine sour cream mixture, remaining ¾ cup sour cream, soup, milk and paprika in same skillet. Cook and stir over medium heat until smooth. *Do not boil.*

4. Spread noodles in prepared dish. Top with meatballs; cover with sauce. Bake 20 minutes or until heated through. Sprinkle with dill, if desired. *Makes 4 to 6 servings*

ARTICHOKE–OLIVE CHICKEN BAKE

1½ cups uncooked rotini pasta
1 tablespoon olive oil
1 medium onion, chopped
1 green bell pepper, chopped
2 cups shredded cooked chicken
1 can (about 14 ounces) diced tomatoes with Italian herbs
1 can (about 14 ounces) artichoke hearts, drained and quartered
1 can (6 ounces) sliced black olives, drained
1 teaspoon Italian seasoning
2 cups (8 ounces) shredded mozzarella cheese

1. Preheat oven to 350°F. Spray 2-quart casserole with nonstick cooking spray.

2. Cook pasta according to package directions until almost tender; drain.

3. Heat oil in large deep skillet over medium heat. Add onion and pepper; cook and stir 1 minute. Add pasta, chicken, tomatoes, artichokes, olives and seasoning; stir until blended.

4. Place half of chicken mixture in prepared casserole; sprinkle with half of cheese. Top with remaining chicken mixture and cheese.

5. Bake, covered, 35 minutes or until hot and bubbly.

Makes 8 servings

MANICOTTI

1 container (15 ounces) ricotta cheese
2 cups (8 ounces) shredded mozzarella cheese
½ cup cottage cheese
2 eggs, beaten
2 tablespoons grated Parmesan cheese
½ teaspoon minced garlic
   Salt and black pepper
1 package (about 8 ounces) uncooked manicotti shells
1 pound ground beef
1 jar (26 ounces) pasta sauce
2 cups water

1. Preheat oven to 375°F.

2. Combine ricotta cheese, mozzarella cheese, cottage cheese, eggs, Parmesan cheese and garlic in large bowl; mix well. Season with salt and pepper. Fill manicotti shells with cheese mixture; place in 13×9-inch baking dish.

3. Brown beef in large skillet over medium-high heat, stirring to break up meat. Drain fat. Stir in pasta sauce and water (mixture will be thin). Pour sauce over filled manicotti shells.

4. Cover with foil. Bake 1 hour or until sauce is thickened and shells are tender.   *Makes 6 servings*

manicotti

ITALIAN TOMATO BAKE

1 pound Italian sausage, cut into ½-inch slices
2 tablespoons butter
1 cup chopped onion
4 cups cooked egg noodles
2 cups frozen broccoli florets, thawed
2 cups pasta sauce
½ cup diced plum tomatoes
2 cloves garlic, minced
3 plum tomatoes, sliced
1 cup ricotta cheese
⅓ cup grated Parmesan cheese
1 teaspoon dried oregano

1. Preheat oven to 350°F. Cook sausage in large skillet over medium heat about 10 minutes or until barely pink in center. Drain sausage on paper towels. Drain fat from skillet.

2. Add butter and onion to skillet; cook and stir until onion is tender. Combine onion, noodles, broccoli, pasta sauce, diced tomatoes and garlic in large bowl; mix well. Transfer to 13×9-inch baking dish.

3. Top with sausage and tomato slices. Place 1 heaping tablespoonful ricotta cheese on each tomato slice. Sprinkle with Parmesan cheese and oregano. Bake 35 minutes or until hot and bubbly.   *Makes 6 servings*

italian tomato bake

SAUSAGE AND BROCCOLI NOODLE CASSEROLE

1 jar (1 pound) RAGÚ® Cheesy! Classic Alfredo Sauce
⅓ cup milk
1 pound sweet Italian sausage, cooked and crumbled
1 package (9 ounces) frozen chopped broccoli, thawed
8 ounces egg noodles, cooked and drained
1 cup shredded Cheddar cheese (about 4 ounces), divided
¼ cup chopped roasted red peppers

1. Preheat oven to 350°F. In large bowl, combine Alfredo Sauce and milk. Stir in sausage, broccoli, noodles, ¾ cup cheese and roasted peppers.

2. In 13×9-inch baking dish, evenly spread sausage mixture. Sprinkle with remaining ¼ cup cheese.

3. Bake 30 minutes or until heated through. *Makes 6 servings*

Tip: Substitute sausage with equal amounts of vegetables for a hearty vegetarian entrée.

Prep Time: 15 minutes
Cook Time: 30 minutes

Italian sausage is available in both links and bulk. Bulk Italian sausage has the same flavorings as Italian sausage links, just without the casings. Whenever a recipe calls for the sausage to be browned and broken up, choose whichever is cheapest. If using links, simply remove the casings before browning the sausage.

sausage and broccoli noodle casserole

SUNDAY SUPPER LASAGNA ROLLS

12 uncooked lasagna noodles
1 pound ground beef
2 onions, chopped
2 red bell peppers, chopped
3 cloves garlic, minced
1 can (28 ounces) diced tomatoes
1 can (8 ounces) tomato sauce
1 can (6 ounces) tomato paste
1 teaspoon dried basil
½ teaspoon dried oregano
   Salt and black pepper
1 container (15 ounces) ricotta cheese
1 package (10 ounces) frozen chopped spinach, thawed and
   squeezed dry
2 cups (8 ounces) shredded Italian cheese blend or mozzarella cheese
1 egg
1 cup (4 ounces) shredded pizza cheese blend or Cheddar cheese

1. Preheat oven to 350°F. Spray 13×9-inch baking dish with nonstick cooking spray. Cook noodles according to package directions; drain.

2. For sauce, brown beef in Dutch oven over medium heat, stirring to break up meat. Drain fat. Add onions, bell peppers and garlic; cook and stir 5 to 7 minutes or until onions are translucent. Add tomatoes, tomato sauce, tomato paste, basil and oregano. Season with salt and black pepper. Cover; simmer 20 minutes or until thickened.

3. Combine ricotta cheese, spinach, Italian cheese blend and egg in large bowl. Season with salt and black pepper.

4. Place 1 noodle on clean work surface. Spread ¼ cup ricotta mixture over half of noodle; top with 3 tablespoons sauce. Roll up noodle jelly-roll style. Place roll seam side down in prepared baking dish. Repeat with remaining noodles. Spoon any remaining ricotta mixture and sauce over rolls. Sprinkle with pizza cheese blend.

5. Cover with foil; bake 30 minutes. Remove foil; bake 15 minutes or until sauce is bubbly and cheese begins to brown.   *Makes 6 servings*

sunday supper lasagna rolls

LEMONY DILL SALMON AND SHELL CASSEROLE

Nonstick cooking spray
1½ cups sliced mushrooms
⅓ cup sliced green onions
1 clove garlic, minced
2 cups milk
3 tablespoons all-purpose flour
1 tablespoon grated lemon peel
¾ teaspoon dried dill weed
¼ teaspoon salt
⅛ teaspoon black pepper
1½ cups frozen peas
1 can (7½ ounces) salmon, drained and flaked
6 ounces uncooked medium shell pasta, cooked and drained

1. Preheat oven to 350°F. Spray 2-quart casserole with cooking spray.

2. Spray medium nonstick saucepan with cooking spray; heat over medium heat. Add mushrooms, green onions and garlic; cook and stir 5 minutes or until vegetables are tender.

3. Whisk milk and flour in medium bowl until smooth. Stir in lemon peel, dill, salt and pepper. Add to mushroom mixture in skillet. Increase heat to medium-high; cook 5 to 8 minutes or until thickened, stirring constantly.

4. Remove from heat. Stir in peas, salmon and pasta. Transfer pasta mixture to prepared casserole. Bake, covered, 35 to 40 minutes or until heated through. Serve immediately.   *Makes 6 servings*

HONEY DIJON CHICKEN & PASTA

1 (3- to 4-pound) chicken, cut up and skinned, if desired
⅓ cup *French's®* Honey Dijon Mustard
⅓ cup Italian salad dressing
1 can (10¾ ounces) condensed cream of chicken soup
4 cups hot cooked rotini pasta (8 ounces uncooked)
1⅓ cups *French's®* French Fried Onions, divided
1 cup diced tomatoes
1 cup diced zucchini
2 tablespoons minced parsley or basil leaves (optional)

1. Preheat oven to 400°F. Place chicken in shallow roasting pan. Mix mustard and dressing. Spoon half of mixture over chicken. Bake, uncovered, 40 minutes.

2. Combine soup, *½ cup water* and remaining mustard mixture. Toss pasta with sauce, *⅔ cup* French Fried Onions, tomatoes, zucchini and parsley. Spoon mixture around chicken.

3. Bake, uncovered, 15 minutes or until chicken is no longer pink in center. Sprinkle with remaining *⅔ cup* onions. Bake 1 minute or until onions are golden. *Makes 6 servings*

Prep Time: 15 minutes
Cook Time: about 1 hour

PASTA AND WHITE BEAN CASSEROLE

    1 tablespoon olive oil
    ½ cup chopped onion
    2 cloves garlic, minced
    2 cans (about 15 ounces each) cannellini beans, rinsed and drained
    3 cups cooked small shell pasta
    1 can (8 ounces) tomato sauce
 1½ teaspoons Italian seasoning
    ½ teaspoon salt
    ½ teaspoon black pepper
    1 cup (4 ounces) shredded Italian cheese blend
    2 tablespoons finely chopped fresh parsley (optional)

1. Preheat oven to 350°F. Spray 2-quart casserole with nonstick cooking spray.

2. Heat oil in large skillet over medium-high heat. Add onion and garlic; cook and stir 3 to 4 minutes or until onion is tender. Stir in beans, pasta, tomato sauce, seasoning, salt and pepper; mix well.

3. Transfer to prepared casserole; sprinkle with cheese blend and parsley, if desired. Bake 20 minutes or until cheese is melted.

Makes 6 servings

Cannellini beans are traditional white beans from Italy. They are sometimes known as white kidney beans. They have a very smooth texture, mellow flavor and maintain their shape well when cooked.

pasta and white bean casserole

CHICKEN NOODLE CASSEROLE

1 can (10¾ ounces) CAMPBELL'S® Condensed Cream of Mushroom Soup (Regular, 98% Fat Free *or* 25% Less Sodium)
½ cup milk
2 tablespoons butter, melted
¼ teaspoon ground black pepper
1 cup frozen broccoli flowerets, thawed
2 cups shredded cooked chicken
2 cups hot cooked medium egg noodles
½ cup grated Parmesan cheese

1. Stir the soup, milk, butter, black pepper, broccoli, chicken and noodles in 2-quart casserole.

2. Bake at 400°F. for 20 minutes or until hot. Stir.

3. Sprinkle with the cheese. Bake for 5 minutes more.

Makes 4 servings

Prep Time: 10 minutes
Bake Time: 25 minutes

chicken noodle casserole

MACARONI & CHEESE WITH BACON

8 ounces uncooked rotini pasta
2 tablespoons butter
2 tablespoons all-purpose flour
¼ teaspoon salt
¼ teaspoon dry mustard
⅛ teaspoon black pepper
1½ cups milk
2 cups (8 ounces) shredded sharp Cheddar cheese
8 ounces bacon, crisp-cooked and crumbled
2 medium tomatoes, sliced

1. Preheat oven to 350°F. Lightly grease shallow 1½-quart casserole.

2. Cook pasta according to package directions; drain and return to saucepan.

3. Melt butter in medium saucepan over medium-low heat. Whisk in flour, salt, mustard and pepper; cook and stir 1 minute. Whisk in milk. Bring to a boil over medium heat, stirring frequently. Reduce heat; simmer 2 minutes. Remove from heat. Add cheese; stir until melted.

4. Add cheese mixture and bacon to pasta; stir until well blended. Transfer to prepared casserole. Bake 20 minutes. Arrange tomato slices on casserole. Bake 5 to 8 minutes or until casserole is bubbly and tomatoes are heated through.   *Makes 4 servings*

macaroni & cheese with bacon

whole grain goodness

MEDITERRANEAN VEGGIE SALAD

    4 ounces uncooked whole wheat rotini pasta
    ½ cup diced seeded tomatoes
    ½ cup thinly sliced zucchini
    ½ cup thinly sliced green bell pepper
    ¼ cup finely chopped red onion
    2 tablespoons coarsely chopped pimiento-stuffed green olives
    2 to 3 teaspoons cider vinegar
    1 teaspoon dried oregano
    ½ teaspoon dried basil
    ½ clove garlic, minced
    1 teaspoon olive oil
    ¼ teaspoon salt
    2 ounces crumbled feta cheese (optional)

1. Cook pasta according to package directions; drain. Rinse under cold water until cool; drain.

2. Meanwhile, combine tomatoes, zucchini, bell pepper, onion, olives, vinegar, oregano, basil and garlic in large bowl; toss to blend.

3. Add pasta, oil and salt to tomato mixture; toss gently. Sprinkle with cheese, if desired. *Makes 2 to 4 servings*

mediterranean veggie salad

GRILLED VEGGIES AND COUSCOUS

⅓ cup pine nuts
1½ cups vegetable broth or water
2 tablespoons olive oil, divided
½ teaspoon salt
1 cup uncooked whole wheat couscous
1 medium zucchini, cut lengthwise into ½-inch slices
1 medium red bell pepper, cut in half
½ small red onion, sliced
¼ cup crumbled feta cheese (optional)
1 clove garlic, minced
½ teaspoon lemon pepper
   Salt and black pepper

1. Toast pine nuts in small nonstick skillet over medium heat
5 minutes or until just brown and fragrant. Let cool.

2. Combine broth, 1 tablespoon oil and salt in small saucepan;
bring to a boil. Stir in couscous. Remove from heat. Cover; let stand
5 minutes or until liquid is absorbed.

3. Prepare grill for direct cooking. Brush vegetables with remaining
1 tablespoon oil. Place vegetables on grid over medium-high heat. Grill
zucchini and onion 3 to 5 minutes or until tender. Grill bell pepper 7 to
10 minutes or until skin is blackened. Place bell pepper in food storage
bag; seal bag. Let stand 3 to 5 minutes. Remove from bag; peel off and
discard blackened skin. Cut vegetables into bite-size pieces.

4. Spoon couscous into serving bowl. Fluff with fork. Add vegetables,
pine nuts, cheese, if desired, garlic and lemon pepper; mix well. Season
with salt and black pepper.   *Makes 4 servings*

grilled veggies and couscous

WHOLE WHEAT PENNE WITH BROCCOLI AND SAUSAGE

6 ounces uncooked whole wheat penne pasta
1 head broccoli, cut into bite-size florets
8 ounces mild Italian sausage, casings removed
1 medium onion, quartered and sliced
2 cloves garlic, minced
2 teaspoons grated lemon peel
¼ teaspoon salt
⅛ teaspoon black pepper
⅓ cup grated Parmesan cheese

1. Cook pasta according to package directions, adding broccoli during last 5 to 6 minutes of cooking. Drain well; cover and keep warm.

2. Meanwhile, heat large skillet over medium heat. Crumble sausage into skillet. Add onion; cook until sausage is brown, stirring to break up meat. Drain fat.

3. Add garlic; cook and stir 1 minute. Add sausage mixture, lemon peel, salt and pepper to pasta; toss until blended. Sprinkle with cheese.   *Makes 4 servings*

whole wheat penne with broccoli and sausage

CARAWAY SWISS STEAK

1 pound boneless beef round steak, trimmed and cut ¾ inch thick
2 tablespoons all-purpose flour
1 teaspoon dried marjoram (optional)
½ teaspoon salt
½ teaspoon black pepper
1 tablespoon canola oil
1 can (about 14 ounces) diced tomatoes
¾ cup beef broth
3 tablespoons tomato paste
2 teaspoons paprika
1 teaspoon caraway seeds
2 cloves garlic, minced
½ cup sour cream
4 cups hot cooked whole wheat noodles

1. Cut steak evenly into 4 pieces. Pound steak pieces to ½ inch thick with meat mallet.

2. Combine flour, marjoram, if desired, salt and pepper in large resealable food storage bag. Add 2 pieces of meat; seal bag. Shake until meat is evenly coated. Repeat with remaining pieces.

3. Heat oil in large nonstick skillet. Add meat; brown on both sides. Combine tomatoes, broth, tomato paste, paprika, caraway seeds and garlic in small bowl. Pour over meat; bring to a boil. Reduce heat; simmer, covered, 60 to 75 minutes or until meat is tender. Skim off fat.

4. Remove meat from skillet. Stir sour cream into tomato mixture. Cook and stir until heated through. *Do not boil.* Serve meat and tomato mixture over hot noodles. *Makes 4 servings*

Prep Time: 20 minutes
Cook Time: 60 to 75 minutes

SWEET & SOUR VEGETABLE COUSCOUS

1 can (about 14 ounces) vegetable broth
1½ cups uncooked whole wheat couscous
1 tablespoon vegetable oil
3 cups frozen Asian blend vegetable mix
⅓ cup stir-fry sauce
2 tablespoons honey
2 tablespoons fresh lemon juice
¼ cup sliced almonds

1. Bring broth to a boil in medium saucepan. Stir in couscous and oil. Remove from heat; cover and let stand 5 minutes or until liquid is absorbed. Fluff couscous with fork; cover to keep warm.

2. Meanwhile, place vegetables in microwavable dish. Microwave according to package directions; drain.

3. Combine stir-fry sauce, honey and lemon juice in small bowl. Pour over cooked vegetables; microwave on HIGH 1 minute.

4. Spoon couscous onto serving plates. Top with vegetable mixture and sprinkle with almonds. *Makes 4 servings*

Tip: For extra flavor and crunch, toast the almonds. Cook and stir almonds in small nonstick skillet over medium heat 2 minutes or until golden brown. Watch carefully to prevent burning.

Prep and Cook Time: 20 minutes

CHICKEN & WALNUT PESTO PASTA SALAD

½ cup fresh basil leaves, packed (about 1 ounce)
¼ cup FISHER® CHEF'S NATURALS® Walnuts, chopped
¼ cup extra virgin olive oil
1 to 2 tablespoons lemon juice
1 tablespoon grated Parmesan cheese
1 small clove garlic, peeled
¾ teaspoon salt
2 ounces uncooked whole wheat rotini pasta
1½ cups asparagus pieces, about 2 inches
2 cups chopped cooked chicken (or precooked diced chicken or rotisserie chicken)
2 cups sliced mushrooms

1. Add basil, walnuts, oil, lemon juice, Parmesan cheese, garlic and salt to blender. Blend, scraping sides and pressing down with rubber spatula frequently.

2. Cook pasta according to directions on package, 6 minutes. Add asparagus, return to a boil and cook 30 seconds or until asparagus is JUST tender crisp. Drain pasta mixture in colander and run under cold water to cool completely. Shake off excess liquid.

3. Place in a large bowl, add basil mixture and remaining ingredients and toss gently, yet thoroughly to coat completely. May add 2 to 3 tablespoons water for a thinner consistency, if desired. Serve immediately for peak flavors.   *Makes 4 servings*

whole grain goodness

chicken & walnut pesto pasta salad

PASTA WITH TUNA, GREEN BEANS & TOMATOES

        8 ounces uncooked whole wheat penne, rigatoni or fusilli pasta
    1½ cups frozen cut green beans, thawed
        3 teaspoons olive oil, divided
        3 green onions, sliced
        1 clove garlic, minced
        1 can (about 14 ounces) diced Italian-style tomatoes, drained
        ½ teaspoon salt
        ½ teaspoon Italian seasoning
        ¼ teaspoon black pepper
        1 can (12 ounces) solid albacore tuna packed in water, drained
            and flaked
        Chopped fresh parsley (optional)

1. Cook pasta according to package directions, adding green beans during last 7 minutes of cooking. Drain.

2. Meanwhile, heat 1 teaspoon oil in large skillet over medium heat. Add green onions and garlic; cook and stir 2 minutes. Add tomatoes, salt, seasoning and pepper; cook and stir 4 to 5 minutes. Add pasta mixture, tuna and remaining 2 teaspoons oil; mix gently until blended. Sprinkle with parsley, if desired.   *Makes 4 to 6 servings*

Canned tuna is precooked and packed in either water or oil. Like other food products, it is available in various quality grades. Solid tuna is more expensive than chunk tuna, however the larger pieces work better in this recipe. Buy less expensive chunk tuna for tuna salad.

pasta with tuna, green beans & tomatoes

VEGETARIAN LASAGNA

1 small eggplant, sliced into ½-inch-thick rounds
½ teaspoon salt
2 tablespoons olive oil, divided
1 tablespoon butter
8 ounces sliced mushrooms
1 small onion, diced
1 jar (26 ounces) pasta sauce
1 teaspoon dried basil
1 teaspoon dried oregano
1 container (15 ounces) ricotta cheese
1½ cups (6 ounces) shredded Monterey Jack cheese
1 cup grated Parmesan cheese, divided
1 package (8 ounces) whole wheat lasagna noodles, cooked
    and drained
1 medium zucchini, thinly sliced

Slow Cooker Directions

1. Sprinkle eggplant with salt; let stand 10 to 15 minutes. Rinse and pat dry. Brush with 1 tablespoon olive oil. Brown both sides in large skillet over medium heat. Set aside.

2. Heat remaining 1 tablespoon olive oil and butter in same skillet over medium heat; cook and stir mushrooms and onion until softened. Stir in pasta sauce, basil and oregano. Set aside.

3. Combine ricotta, Monterey Jack and ½ cup Parmesan cheese in medium bowl. Set aside.

4. Spread one third of sauce mixture in bottom of slow cooker. Layer with one third of lasagna noodles, half of eggplant and half of cheese mixture. Repeat layers once. Top with remaining third of lasagna noodles, zucchini and remaining third of sauce mixture. Sprinkle with remaining ½ cup Parmesan cheese.

5. Cover; cook on LOW 6 hours. Let stand 15 to 20 minutes before serving. *Makes 4 to 6 servings*

SALMON AND GREEN BEAN SALAD WITH PASTA

1 can (6 ounces) red or pink salmon
8 ounces uncooked whole wheat small shell pasta
¾ cup green beans, cut into 2-inch pieces
⅔ cup shredded carrots
½ cup cottage cheese
3 tablespoons plain yogurt
1½ tablespoons fresh lemon juice
1 tablespoon chopped fresh dill
2 teaspoons grated onion
1 teaspoon Dijon mustard

1. Drain salmon and separate into chunks; set aside.

2. Cook pasta according to package directions, adding green beans during last 3 minutes of cooking; drain. Rinse under cold water until cool; drain.

3. Combine pasta mixture, carrots and salmon in medium bowl.

4. Place cottage cheese, yogurt, lemon juice, dill, onion and mustard in food processor or blender; process until smooth. Pour over pasta mixture; toss to coat evenly.   *Makes 4 to 6 servings*

Canned salmon is either red or pink. Red salmon is more expensive with a firm texture and deep color. Pink salmon is less expensive with a lighter flavor and color than the red variety. Choose either variety for this recipe.

MEDITERRANEAN ARTICHOKE SALAD WITH ROTINI

8 ounces uncooked whole wheat rotini pasta
1 can (about 14 ounces) artichoke hearts, rinsed, drained and coarsely
   chopped
1 package (8 ounces) mushrooms, thinly sliced
1 medium tomato, chopped
1 small red onion, finely chopped
8 kalamata olives, coarsely chopped
¼ cup chopped fresh parsley
3 tablespoons white wine vinegar
1 clove garlic, minced
1 ounce crumbled feta cheese (optional)

1. Cook pasta according to package directions; drain. Rinse under cold water until cool; drain.

2. Combine pasta, artichokes, mushrooms, tomato, onion, olives, parsley, vinegar and garlic in medium bowl; toss to blend. Sprinkle with cheese, if desired.

3. Let stand 15 minutes. Serve immediately or cover and refrigerate up to 4 hours. *Makes 4 servings*

WHOLE WHEAT SPAGHETTI WITH CAULIFLOWER & FETA

3 tablespoons olive oil
1 onion, chopped
4 cloves garlic, minced
1 head cauliflower, cut into bite-size florets
⅔ cup vegetable broth or water
1 teaspoon salt
½ teaspoon black pepper
8 ounces uncooked whole wheat spaghetti
1 pint grape tomatoes, cut in half
½ cup coarsely chopped walnuts
¼ teaspoon red pepper flakes (optional)
½ cup crumbled feta cheese

1. Heat oil in large skillet over medium heat. Add onion; cook and stir 3 minutes or until soft. Add garlic; cook and stir 2 minutes. Add cauliflower; cook and stir 5 minutes. Add broth, salt and black pepper. Cover; cook 15 minutes or until cauliflower is crisp-tender.

2. Meanwhile, cook pasta according to package directions. Drain, reserving ½ cup pasta cooking water. Keep pasta warm.

3. Add tomatoes, walnuts, reserved pasta water and pepper flakes, if desired, to skillet. Cook 2 to 3 minutes or until tomatoes begin to soften.

4. Toss pasta with cauliflower mixture in skillet or serving bowl; sprinkle with cheese. *Makes 4 servings*

whole wheat spaghetti with cauliflower & feta

FRESH SPINACH AND COUSCOUS SALAD WITH FETA CHEESE

1½ cups water
  1 cup uncooked whole wheat couscous
  1 can (about 15 ounces) white beans, rinsed and drained
  1 cup packed chopped stemmed spinach
  3 slices (1 ounce) hard salami, cut into thin strips
  1 can (2¼ ounces) sliced black olives, drained
  1 tablespoon dried oregano
1½ teaspoons dried basil
  ⅛ teaspoon red pepper flakes
  3 tablespoons vinaigrette dressing
  3 tablespoons cider vinegar
  3 ounces crumbled feta cheese

Microwave Directions

1. Microwave water in medium microwavable bowl on HIGH 2 to 3 minutes or until boiling. Stir in couscous. Cover with plastic wrap; let stand 5 minutes or until liquid is absorbed.

2. Place couscous in fine mesh strainer. Rinse under cold water until cool; drain.

3. Combine beans, spinach, salami, olives, oregano, basil, pepper flakes, dressing and vinegar in large bowl; mix well.

4. Add couscous to spinach mixture; mix well. Add cheese; toss gently.

Makes 4 servings

fresh spinach and couscous salad
with feta cheese

6 ingredients or less

FETTUCCINE GORGONZOLA WITH SUN–DRIED TOMATOES

4 ounces sun-dried tomatoes (not packed in oil)
8 ounces uncooked spinach or tri-color fettuccine
1 cup cottage cheese
½ cup plain yogurt
½ cup (2 ounces) crumbled Gorgonzola cheese
⅛ teaspoon black pepper
Additional crumbled Gorgonzola cheese (optional)

1. Place sun-dried tomatoes in small bowl; pour hot water over to cover. Let stand 15 minutes or until tomatoes are soft; drain. Cut tomatoes into strips.

2. Cook pasta according to package directions; drain. Cover and keep warm.

3. Meanwhile, process cottage cheese and yogurt in food processor or blender until smooth. Heat cottage cheese mixture in large skillet over low heat. Add Gorgonzola cheese and pepper; stir until cheese is melted.

4. Add pasta and tomatoes to skillet; toss to coat with sauce. Sprinkle with additional Gorgonzola cheese, if desired. Serve immediately.

Makes 4 servings

fettuccine gorgonzola with sun-dried tomatoes

SIMPLY DELICIOUS PASTA PRIMAVERA

¼ cup I CAN'T BELIEVE IT'S NOT BUTTER!® Spread
1 envelope LIPTON® RECIPE SECRETS® Vegetable Soup Mix
1½ cups milk
8 ounces linguine or spaghetti, cooked and drained
¼ cup grated Parmesan cheese (about 1 ounce)

1. In medium saucepan, melt spread over medium heat; stir in soup mix and milk. Bring just to a boil over high heat.

2. Reduce heat to low and simmer uncovered, stirring occasionally, 10 minutes or until vegetables are tender. Toss hot linguine with sauce and Parmesan cheese.   *Makes 4 servings*

Prep Time: 5 minutes
Cook Time: 12 minutes

 Dry soup mix is the superstar of the budget-conscious shopper's pantry. These inexpensive envelopes of seasonings come in a wide variety of flavors and take up little space on the shelf. They can be combined with sour cream or yogurt to make a savory party dip, blended with just enough olive oil to make a paste for marinating chicken or pork, or heated with undiluted condensed soup to make a creamy sauce for a roast.

6 ingredients or less

SPICY SAUSAGE MAC & CHEESE BAKE

   3 hot Italian sausage links (about 1 pound)
  ¼ cup water
   1 package (14 ounces) deluxe macaroni and cheese dinner
     Salt and black pepper
1½ cups (6 ounces) shredded sharp Cheddar cheese

1. Preheat oven to 350°F. Spray 2-quart baking dish with nonstick cooking spray.

2. Place sausages in medium nonstick skillet; add water. Heat over medium heat; cover and simmer 10 to 12 minutes, turning once. Remove cover; brown sausages on all sides. Remove from heat. When cool enough to handle, cut sausages in half lengthwise and then into ½-inch pieces.

3. Prepare macaroni and cheese according to package directions. Stir in sausage pieces. Season with salt and pepper.

4. Spoon half of macaroni mixture into prepared baking dish. Sprinkle with half of cheese. Top with remaining half of macaroni mixture and remaining half of cheese. Bake 10 to 12 minutes or until heated through. *Makes 4 to 6 servings*

spicy sausage mac & cheese bake

PENNSYLVANIA DUTCH HAM & NOODLE CASSEROLE

1 tablespoon vegetable oil
2 cups cubed cooked ham (about 1 pound)
1 medium onion, chopped (about ½ cup)
1 can (10¾ ounces) CAMPBELL'S® Condensed Cream of Mushroom Soup
    (Regular *or* 98% Fat Free)
8 ounces extra-sharp Cheddar cheese, sliced
8 ounces extra-wide egg noodles (2 cups), cooked and drained

1. Heat the oil in a 4-quart saucepan over medium-high heat. Add the ham and onion and cook until the onion is tender.

2. Stir the soup into the saucepan. Reduce the heat to medium. Cook and stir for 5 minutes. Add the cheese and stir until the cheese melts. Gently stir in the noodles. Heat through, stirring often.

Makes 4 servings

Easy Substitution Tip: Substitute cooked chicken or turkey for the ham.

Start to Finish Time: 25 minutes
Prepping: 10 minutes
Cooking: 15 minutes

pennsylvania dutch ham & noodle casserole

BOW TIE PASTA WITH SAVORY LENTIL SAUCE

  1 can (13¾ ounces) chicken broth
  ½ cup water
  ½ cup dry lentils, rinsed and drained
  1 jar (1 pound 10 ounces) RAGÚ® Light Pasta Sauce
  1 tablespoon balsamic vinegar
  1 box (16 ounces) bow tie pasta, cooked and drained

In 3-quart saucepot or Dutch oven, bring chicken broth, water and lentils to a boil over high heat. Reduce heat to low and simmer covered, stirring occasionally, 20 minutes. Stir in Pasta Sauce and vinegar. Simmer covered, stirring occasionally, an additional 20 minutes or until lentils are tender. Serve over hot pasta.

Makes 8 servings

PASTA WITH RED CLAM SAUCE

  1 tablespoon vegetable oil
  2 cans (6½ ounces each) chopped clams, rinsed and drained
  1 jar (26 ounces) chunky marinara or tomato sauce
  1 package (9 ounces) frozen peas
  1 pound linguine, cooked and drained

1. Combine oil and clams in large pan over medium heat. Cook and stir 5 minutes or until clams begin to sizzle. Add marinara sauce; bring to a boil. Reduce heat; simmer 15 to 20 minutes or until sauce is slightly reduced.

2. Add frozen peas; cook 5 minutes or until cooked through. Divide pasta equally among 6 bowls; serve sauce over pasta.

Makes 6 servings

6 ingredients or less

CHEESEBURGER MACARONI

- 1 cup mostaccioli or elbow macaroni, uncooked
- 1 pound ground beef
- 1 medium onion, chopped
- 1 can (14½ ounces) DEL MONTE® Diced Tomatoes with Basil, Garlic & Oregano
- ¼ cup DEL MONTE® Tomato Ketchup
- 1 cup (4 ounces) shredded Cheddar cheese

1. Cook pasta according to package directions; drain.

2. Brown meat with onion in large skillet; drain. Season with salt and pepper, if desired. Stir in undrained tomatoes, ketchup and pasta; heat through.

3. Top with cheese. Garnish, if desired.   *Makes 4 servings*

ROSEMARY CHICKEN LINGUINE WITH BABY CARROTS

- ¼ cup milk
- 2 tablespoons margarine or butter
- 1 (4.7-ounce) package PASTA RONI® Chicken & Broccoli Flavor with Linguine
- 1 pound boneless, skinless chicken breasts, cut into 1-inch pieces
- 1½ cups fresh or frozen baby carrots, thawed
- ¼ teaspoon dried rosemary, crushed

1. In large saucepan, bring 1⅔ cups water, milk and margarine to a boil.

2. Stir in pasta, chicken, carrots, rosemary and Special Seasonings; return to a boil. Reduce heat to medium. Gently boil uncovered, 9 to 10 minutes or until pasta is tender, stirring occasionally. Let stand 5 minutes before serving.   *Makes 4 servings*

SHELLS AND GORGONZOLA

 1 pound uncooked medium shell pasta
 1 jar (24 ounces) vodka sauce
 1 package (4 ounces) crumbled Gorgonzola cheese

1. Cook pasta according to package directions; drain.

2. Meanwhile, heat sauce in medium saucepan over medium heat.

3. Drain pasta; return to saucepan. Stir sauce into pasta. Stir in cheese just before serving. *Makes 4 to 6 servings*

Variation: Add 2 cups packed torn spinach to hot drained pasta before adding sauce.

PENNE WITH EGGPLANT AND TURKEY SAUSAGE

 1 pound Italian turkey sausage, cut into 1-inch pieces
 1 medium eggplant, cut into ½-inch cubes
 4 cups prepared chunky vegetable spaghetti sauce
12 ounces penne pasta, cooked according to package directions and drained
 4 ounces Asiago cheese, grated

1. In large nonstick skillet, over medium heat, sauté turkey sausage and eggplant 12 to 15 minutes or until sausage is no longer pink and eggplant is soft and lightly browned. Add spaghetti sauce to turkey mixture and simmer 3 minutes or until heated through.

2. To serve, spoon sauce over drained penne and top with cheese.
Makes 8 servings

Favorite recipe from *National Turkey Federation*

shells and gorgonzola

CHICKEN AND VEGETABLE PASTA

8 ounces uncooked bowtie pasta
1 pound boneless skinless chicken breasts
2 red or green bell peppers, cut into quarters
1 medium zucchini, cut in half
½ cup Italian dressing
½ cup prepared pesto

1. Cook pasta according to package directions; drain. Cover and keep warm.

2. Combine chicken, peppers, zucchini and dressing in medium bowl; toss well.

3. Prepare grill for direct cooking or preheat broiler.

4. Grill or broil chicken and vegetables 12 minutes or until chicken is no longer pink in center and vegetables are crisp-tender, turning once.

5. Cut vegetables and chicken into bite-size pieces. Combine pasta, chicken, vegetables and pesto in large bowl; toss well.

Makes 4 to 6 servings

Prep and Cook Time: 20 minutes

chicken and vegetable pasta

TURKEY SAUSAGE & PASTA TOSS

8 ounces uncooked penne or gemelli pasta
1 can (about 14 ounces) stewed tomatoes
6 ounces turkey kielbasa or smoked turkey sausage
2 cups (1-inch) asparagus pieces or broccoli florets
2 tablespoons prepared pesto
2 tablespoons grated Parmesan cheese

1. Cook pasta according to package directions; drain.

2. Meanwhile, heat tomatoes in medium saucepan over medium heat. Cut sausage into ¼-inch-thick slices; add to tomatoes. Stir in asparagus and pesto; cover and simmer 6 minutes or until asparagus is crisp-tender.

3. Toss pasta with tomato mixture; sprinkle with cheese.

Makes 4 servings

FUSILLI WITH BROCCOLI RABE

8 ounces uncooked fusilli pasta
1 pound broccoli rabe, trimmed and cut into 1-inch pieces
⅓ cup FILIPPO BERIO® Extra Virgin Olive Oil
1 clove garlic, minced
Salt and freshly ground black pepper
Grated pecorino cheese

Cook pasta according to package directions until al dente (tender but still firm). Drain. In large saucepan, cook broccoli rabe in boiling salted water 3 minutes or until tender. Add to colander with pasta. Drain; transfer to large bowl. In small saucepan, heat olive oil over medium heat until hot. Add garlic; cook and stir 30 seconds to 1 minute or until golden. Add to pasta mixture; toss until well coated. Season to taste with salt and pepper. Top with cheese.

Makes 3 to 4 servings

6 ingredients or less

QUICK PASTA WITH PEPPERS

    8 ounces uncooked penne or rigatoni pasta
    2 tablespoons olive oil
    1 *each* red, yellow and green bell pepper, thinly sliced
    1 jar (26 ounces) marinara sauce
    ¼ cup grated Parmesan cheese

1. Cook pasta according to package directions; drain. Cover and keep warm.

2. Meanwhile, heat oil in large skillet over medium-high heat. Add bell peppers; cook and stir 2 minutes. Reduce heat to medium; stir in sauce. Cook and stir 5 minutes or until heated through.

3. Pour sauce over hot pasta; sprinkle with cheese before serving.

Makes 6 servings

Variation: Add 1 cup coarsely chopped pepperoni to the sauce.

VEG•ALL® BEEF & CHEDDAR BAKE

    2 cans (15 ounces each) VEG•ALL® Original Mixed Vegetables, drained
    3 cups shredded Cheddar cheese
    2 cups cooked elbow macaroni
    1 pound extra-lean ground beef, cooked and drained
    ½ cup chopped onion
    ¼ teaspoon black pepper

1. Preheat oven to 350°F.

2. In large mixing bowl, combine Veg•All, cheese, macaroni, ground beef, onion and pepper; mix well. Pour mixture into large casserole.

3. Bake for 30 to 35 minutes. Serve hot.

Makes 4 to 6 servings

RAGÚ® FETTUCCINE CARBONARA

1 box (12 ounces) fettuccine
1 cup frozen green peas
1 jar (1 pound) RAGÚ® Cheesy! Classic Alfredo Sauce
4 slices bacon, crisp-cooked and crumbled

1. Cook fettuccine according to package directions, adding peas during last 2 minutes of cooking; drain and set aside.

2. In 2-quart saucepan, heat Alfredo Sauce; stir in bacon.

3. To serve, toss Alfredo Sauce with hot fettuccine and peas. Sprinkle, if desired, with ground black pepper and grated Parmesan cheese.

Makes 6 servings

Prep Time: 5 minutes
Cook Time: 20 minutes

SOUTHWESTERN SKILLET MACARONI

1½ cups uncooked elbow macaroni
1 pound ground beef
¼ cup chili powder
1 can (28 ounces) crushed tomatoes in purée
⅓ cup *Frank's® RedHot®* Original Cayenne Pepper Sauce
1 cup (4 ounces) shredded Cheddar cheese

1. Cook macaroni in boiling water 5 minutes. Drain.

2. In large nonstick skillet, cook ground beef with chili powder until meat is browned. Add tomatoes and **Frank's RedHot** Sauce. Heat to boiling. Reduce heat to medium. Cook 5 minutes.

3. Add macaroni; cook 5 minutes or until pasta is tender and has absorbed excess liquid. Sprinkle with cheese.

Makes 4 servings

ragú® fettuccine carbonara

CHICKEN WITH ROASTED GARLIC SAUCE

1 teaspoon olive oil
4 boneless skinless chicken breasts
1 jar (about 28 ounces) roasted garlic pasta sauce
1 cup sliced mushrooms
8 ounces rotini or fusilli pasta, cooked and drained
   Grated Parmesan cheese (optional)

1. Heat oil in large skillet over medium heat. Brown chicken on both sides. Remove from skillet; cut into thin strips. Return to skillet.

2. Stir in pasta sauce and mushrooms. Cover; simmer 10 minutes or until chicken is cooked through. Stir in pasta. Sprinkle with cheese, if desired. *Makes 4 servings*

PIZZA CASSEROLE

1 pound BOB EVANS® Italian Roll Sausage
12 ounces wide noodles, cooked according to package directions
2 (14-ounce) jars pepperoni pizza sauce
2 cups (8 ounces) shredded Cheddar cheese
2 cups (8 ounces) shredded mozzarella cheese
6 ounces sliced pepperoni

Preheat oven to 350°F. Crumble and cook sausage in medium skillet over medium heat until browned. Drain on paper towels. Layer half of noodles in lightly greased 13×9-inch casserole dish. Top with half of sausage, half of pizza sauce, half of cheeses and half of pepperoni. Repeat layers with remaining ingredients, reserving several pepperoni slices for garnish on top of casserole. Bake 35 to 40 minutes. Refrigerate leftovers. *Makes 6 to 8 servings*

chicken with roasted garlic sauce

CHEESY STUFFED MEATBALLS & SPAGHETTI

1 pound ground beef
½ cup Italian seasoned dry bread crumbs
1 egg
2 ounces mozzarella cheese, cut into 12 (½-inch) cubes
1 jar (1 pound 10 ounces) RAGÚ® Old World Style® Pasta Sauce
8 ounces spaghetti, cooked and drained

1. In medium bowl, combine ground beef, bread crumbs and egg; shape into 12 meatballs. Press 1 cheese cube into each meatball, enclosing completely.

2. In 3-quart saucepan, bring Pasta Sauce to a boil over medium-high heat. Gently stir in uncooked meatballs.

3. Reduce heat to low and simmer covered, stirring occasionally, 20 minutes or until meatballs are done. Serve over hot spaghetti. Sprinkle, if desired, with grated Parmesan cheese. *Makes 4 servings*

Prep Time: 20 minutes
Cook Time: 20 minutes

Make spaghetti and meatballs more exciting with this family-friendly recipe. Everyone will love the delicious cheesy surprise in the center of each meatball.

cheesy stuffed meatballs & spaghetti

ACKNOWLEDGMENTS

The publisher would like to thank the companies and organizations listed below for the use of their recipes and photographs in this publication.

Bob Evans®

Campbell Soup Company

Del Monte Corporation

Filippo Berio® Olive Oil

Fisher® Nuts

The Golden Grain Company®

National Turkey Federation

North Dakota Wheat Commission

Reckitt Benckiser Inc.

Unilever

Veg•All®

INDEX

METRIC CONVERSION CHART

VOLUME MEASUREMENTS (dry)

1/8 teaspoon = 0.5 mL
1/4 teaspoon = 1 mL
1/2 teaspoon = 2 mL
3/4 teaspoon = 4 mL
1 teaspoon = 5 mL
1 tablespoon = 15 mL
2 tablespoons = 30 mL
1/4 cup = 60 mL
1/3 cup = 75 mL
1/2 cup = 125 mL
2/3 cup = 150 mL
3/4 cup = 175 mL
1 cup = 250 mL
2 cups = 1 pint = 500 mL
3 cups = 750 mL
4 cups = 1 quart = 1 L

VOLUME MEASUREMENTS (fluid)

1 fluid ounce (2 tablespoons) = 30 mL
4 fluid ounces (1/2 cup) = 125 mL
8 fluid ounces (1 cup) = 250 mL
12 fluid ounces (1 1/2 cups) = 375 mL
16 fluid ounces (2 cups) = 500 mL

WEIGHTS (mass)

1/2 ounce = 15 g
1 ounce = 30 g
3 ounces = 90 g
4 ounces = 120 g
8 ounces = 225 g
10 ounces = 285 g
12 ounces = 360 g
16 ounces = 1 pound = 450 g

DIMENSIONS

1/16 inch = 2 mm
1/8 inch = 3 mm
1/4 inch = 6 mm
1/2 inch = 1.5 cm
3/4 inch = 2 cm
1 inch = 2.5 cm

OVEN TEMPERATURES

250°F = 120°C
275°F = 140°C
300°F = 150°C
325°F = 160°C
350°F = 180°C
375°F = 190°C
400°F = 200°C
425°F = 220°C
450°F = 230°C

BAKING PAN SIZES

Utensil	Size in Inches/Quarts	Metric Volume	Size in Centimeters
Baking or Cake Pan (square or rectangular)	8×8×2	2 L	20×20×5
	9×9×2	2.5 L	23×23×5
	12×8×2	3 L	30×20×5
	13×9×2	3.5 L	33×23×5
Loaf Pan	8×4×3	1.5 L	20×10×7
	9×5×3	2 L	23×13×7
Round Layer Cake Pan	8×1½	1.2 L	20×4
	9×1½	1.5 L	23×4
Pie Plate	8×1¼	750 mL	20×3
	9×1¼	1 L	23×3
Baking Dish or Casserole	1 quart	1 L	—
	1½ quart	1.5 L	—
	2 quart	2 L	—